STOP PROCRASTINATING: GET TO WORK!

James R. Sherman, Ph.D.

CRISP PUBLICATIONS, INC.
Los Altos, California

STOP PROCRASTINATING: GET TO WORK!

James R. Sherman, Ph.D.

CREDITS
Editors: **Michael G. Crisp**
Designer: **Carol Harris**
Typesetting: **Interface Studio**
Cover Design: **Carol Harris**
Artwork: **Ralph Mapson**

Copyright © 1989 by Crisp Publications, Inc.
Printed in the United States of America

Crisp books are distributed in Canada by Reid Publishing, Ltd., P.O. Box 7267, Oakville, Ontario, Canada L6J 6L6.

In Australia by Career Builders, P.O. Box 1051 Springwood, Brisbane, Queensland, Australia 4127.

And in New Zealand by Career Builders, P.O. Box 571, Manurewa, New Zealand.

Library of Congress Catalog Card Number 89-90837
Sherman, James R.
Stop Procrastinating: Get To Work!
ISBN 0-931961-88-2

INTRODUCTION

Congratulations! You took your first step toward breaking the procrastination habit when you picked up this book. If you keep working at it, you will bring about some very significant changes in your life simply by following the advice in these pages.

One way to keep your momentum going is by discovering some background information about this good-for-nothing habit you're trying to get rid of.

WHAT IS IT?

Procrastination is the intentional and habitual postponement of some important task that should be done.

Another way of defining it is that it is "the art of keeping up with yesterday."

WHAT'S WRONG WITH PROCRASTINATING?

1. It's a lousy habit that can affect you both mentally and physically. Most procrastinators suffer stress, tension, anxiety, and fatigue.
2. It can put the "kabosh" on your life goals and objectives.
3. It stifles your personal and professional growth and keeps you from getting the rewards that should be rightfully yours.
4. It can destroy your dreams of living a happy, healthy, and prosperous life.

WHAT ARE THE CONSEQUENCES?

Procrastination slams the brakes on the wheels of progress. It chews up goals and aspirations and spits out frustration, anger, and despair. You can see its damaging effects in people who stay too long in the wrong job or wrong relationship. You can see it in people who refuse to deal with their abuse of diets, drugs, (including alcohol), or tobacco. And you can see it in people who avoid arduous tasks and unpleasant confrontations until it's too late to take effective action.

You, like most others, have high aspirations for success and a strong desire to achieve your hoped-for goals. The stronger your desires, the greater your frustration and anger will be if you do not satisfy them; especially when procrastination stands in your way.

Good Luck!

James R. Sherman

James R. Sherman

i

ABOUT THIS BOOK

STOP PROCRASTINATING: GET TO WORK! is not like most books. It stands out from other self-help books in an important way. It's not a book to read—it's a book to *use.* The unique ''self-paced'' format of this book and the many cases and worksheets encourage the reader to get involved and try some new ideas immediately.

The simple yet sound concepts and techniques presented will help readers understand the causes of procrastination and will help them learn to take action and become more successful both in their careers and personal lives.

STOP PROCRASTINATING (and other titles listed in the back of this book) can be used effectively in a number of ways. Here are some possibilities:

—**Individual Study.** Because the book is self-instructional, all that is needed is a quiet place, some time, and a pencil. By completing the activities and exercises, a reader should not only receive valuable feedback, but also practical steps for self-improvement.

—**Workshops and Seminars.** The book is ideal for assigned reading prior to a workshop or seminar. With the basics in hand, the quality of the participation will improve, and more time can be spent on concept extensions and applications during the program. The book is also effective when it is distributed at the beginning of a session, and participants ''work through'' the contents.

—**Remote Location Training.** Books can be sent to those not able to attend ''home office'' training sessions.

There are several other possibilities that depend on the objectives, program, or ideas of the user.

One thing for sure, even after it has been read, this book will be looked at—and thought about—again and again.

TABLE OF CONTENTS

INTRODUCTION i

ABOUT THIS BOOK ii

SECTION I—ARE YOU A PROCRASTINATOR?

Are You A Procrastinator? 2

If You Don't Feel Guilty You Aren't Procrastinating! .3

How To Stop Procrastinating For Good 4

What's Ahead 5

SECTION II—WHY PEOPLE PROCRASTINATE

Why People Procrastinate 8

What Causes Me To Procrastinate? 9

Major Causes Of Procrastination 10

SECTION III—HOW TO STOP PROCRASTINATING

How To Stop Procrastinating 30

Get Off Your Duff 31

Suggestions To Stop Procrastinating 32

SECTION IV—YOUR PLAN OF ACTION

Start Planning Now! 54

Establish A Goal 56

SECTION I

ARE YOU A PROCRASTINATOR?

ARE YOU A PROCRASTINATOR?

Millions of people, with otherwise good intentions, postpone important things they know they should be doing. You're one of them if you respond positively to each of the following statements: (Be truthful.)

1. I know who and what I am...but I want something better!

2. I'm frustrated because I can't do everythng I want to do.

3. I'm delaying an important task I know I should be working on and that bothers me. (Your task could be: asking for a raise, finishing a report, calling on a prospect, starting a new career, studying for an examination, etc.). Add your own:

   My Task: _____

4. My task is important because this is what will happen if I don't do it:

   The Consequence: _____

   _____

5. My task has a beginning, an ending, and a definite outcome. (e.g., making a sale, getting a raise, producing a document)

   The Beginning: _____

   The Ending: _____

   The Specific Outcome: _____

6. There is a specific day, month, hour, or year on which I hope to have my task completed and I know what's early and what's late.

   The Completion date: _____

7. I am deliberately doing something else to avoid my task. (e.g., eating, drinking, sleeping, playing dead, playing tennis, doing busywork.)...Add your own:

   My Delaying tactics: _____

   _____

8. I know in my heart that I really should be doing this task and I feel guilty about not doing it.

   Yes _____   No _____

IF YOU DON'T FEEL GUILTY, YOU AREN'T PROCRASTINATING

A little anxiety about goofing off can develop into painful depression if you're sincerely into procrastination. But generally you'll just sweat a little when you postpone a sales call or try to avoid a confrontation with your boss.

If you don't feel guilty, you're probably just being selective about the things you choose to do. In other words, you're not procrastinating about getting your reports done if you think it's most important to call on customers, even if someone else thinks the reports should come first.

Are you a procrastinator? The formula is pretty simple:

A = You postpone things you should be doing
B = You feel guilty about doing it

A + B = Procrastinator

IF YOU DON'T FEEL GUILTY– YOU'RE NOT PROCRASTINATING

HOW TO STOP PROCRASTINATING FOR GOOD

Are you angry and frustrated? Do you routinely have delays and postponements that keep you from reaching your goals and objectives? If so, then here's a simple, straightforward procedure that will help you break the procrastination habit and get you moving on the road to success.

Take these four easy steps and put an end to procrastination once and for all:

1. Acknowledge the simple fact that you procrastinate. Then make up your mind to stop doing it.
   I have procrastinated in the past, but I'm not going to do it anymore.

   Signed: _____

   Date: _____

2. Learn as much as you can about procrastination.
   • Recognize what it is.
   • Figure out why you do it.
   • Find out what you can do to stop.

3. Make a list of specific things you're going to start doing right away to break this lousy habit.

   First, I'm going to: _____

   Then, I'll: _____

   Finally, I'll: _____

4. Carry out your plan of action.

"Try not," said Yoda, the Jedi Master. "Do. Or do not. There is no try."
"The Empire Strikes Back"
George Lucas

Commit yourself to getting rid of procrastination and do it now!

WHAT'S AHEAD

Jump into Section II and you'll find fifteen of the most common causes of procrastination. Move to Section III, and you'll discover eighteen of the best things you can do to break this depressing habit and start getting things done. When you get to Section IV, you'll find a way to put it all together in a personalized plan for the future.

If you think you already know why you procrastinate, you might be tempted to skip the next section. Don't! You might be surprised. Take some time and check it out. The more you know about the causes of procrastination, the easier it will be to break away from the steely grip it has on you.

SECTION II

WHY PEOPLE PROCRASTINATE

WHY PEOPLE PROCRASTINATE

People procrastinate for lots of reasons. Psychologists often say it's because of frustration, insecurity, or fear of failure. But those are just a few of the things that can bring on delays and postponements.

Sometimes a subconscious fear keeps people from taking action. Especially when they know they should be doing something, but are unable to do it and can't figure out why.

Many people think procrastination is no big deal. Accordingly, they don't worry about what causes it. They think they can break the habit whenever they want. However, any reason should be considered serious if it keeps people from reaching their dreams of success.

If you're like most procrastinators, you're actively concerned about the things you do. And you'd like to do better than you're doing right now. You recognize and understand some of the major causes of your procrastination, but there are others that you just can't put your finger on. That's where the following exercise will help.

On the facing page write down at least ten reasons why you procrastinate. Then, as you go through this section, compare your list with the causes that are presented. You may find causes that aren't on your list. Or you may have listed some that aren't included here. That's okay. This section includes the most common causes, not necessarily the prizewinners.

WHAT CAUSES ME TO PROCRASTINATE

(BE HONEST—YOU'RE NOT FOOLING ANYONE BUT YOURSELF)

1.

_____

2.

_____

3.

_____

4.

_____

5.

_____

6.

_____

7.

_____

8.

_____

9.

_____

10.

_____

MAJOR CAUSES OF PROCRASTINATION

The causes that follow in this section aren't listed in any particular order of magnitude or importance. You can decide how important they are after you've figured out how they affect you.

Following is a list of major causes. Check any that apply to you and then read the case examples to see if you can identify yourself. I procrastinate because of:

- ☐ Confusion
- ☐ Lack of Priorities
- ☐ Lack of Responsibility
- ☐ Fear of Risk-Taking
- ☐ Escape from Unpleasant Tasks
- ☐ Anxiety or Depression
- ☐ Obsessive/Compulsive Behavior
- ☐ Monotony or Boredom
- ☐ Fatigue
- ☐ Outside Distractions
- ☐ Lack of Analytical Ability
- ☐ Forgetfulness
- ☐ Dependence on Others
- ☐ Manipulation of Others
- ☐ Physical Disabilities

ADD YOUR OWN:

- ☐
- ☐

#1 CONFUSION

Whenever Jessica runs into a big, complex task, she gets confused and uncertain about what to do next. She sees a multitude of starting places, but can't decide where to start. She's afraid she'll make a mistake no matter what she chooses to do. She wishes her task would somehow shrink to the point where she knows where to start without making any mistakes.

Jessica knows (deep down inside) that if she makes a mistake she can start over and try something else. She also knows that restarting takes time. And the size of her task tells her that time is already scarce. So instead of doing something that will get her started, she does nothing.

Has confusion ever caused you to procrastinate? If so, write a brief description of what the circumstances were in the space provided below:

MAJOR CAUSES OF PROCRASTINATION (Continued)

#2 LACK OF PRIORITIES

Michael has no sense of urgency about what ought to be done first. He jumps from task to task and can't understand why he gets so little done. He also finds it difficult to say ''no'' to new tasks whenever they come along. That's because he can't tell the difference between what's important and what's not. He gives his time and energy to anything and everything he sees in front of him. The result is, he ends up with too much to do and no organized way of doing it. Things keep piling up on his desk and while he tries to find a way through the mess, his dreams of success fade like morning mist.

Has a lack of priorities ever caused you to procrastinate? If so, write a brief summary of what happened in the space below:

#3 LACK OF RESPONSIBILITY

Jennifer procrastinates by refusing to accept responsibility. She says she can't get anything done because current conditions aren't acceptable. She also rationalizes her delays by blaming other people for causing those unacceptable conditions.

Jennifer is not unique. Some students stay in college instead of getting a job, then they blame Congress for causing job shortages. Some employees shy away from promotions and additional responsibilities because they claim that the jobs don't pay enough. Some people prolong or invent physical ailments to avoid going back to work, then they criticize their doctors for not curing them.

Jennifer will keep procrastinating until she's willing to be accountable for her actions and assume responsibility for her own destiny.

Have you ever postponed taking action because you refused to accept responsibility? If so, don't procrastinate! Write your personal examples in the space provided:

MAJOR CAUSES OF PROCRASTINATION (Continued)

#4 FEARS OF RISK-TAKING

Andrew is afraid to take risks. He wants everything to stay the way it is. He procrastinates to protect himself from the unpredictable consequences of developing new clients, taking on new assignments, or moving into new marketing areas. He feels it's better to do nothing than to accept change and possibly make mistakes.

The dangers Andrew sees—whether real or make-believe—may be mental, physical, social, or economic. Since Andrew tends to exaggerate those dangers, they've grown way out of proportion. All that it does is compound his problem because the greater the perceived risk, the longer the delay.

Unless Andrew stops procrastinating and accepts risk as a natural part of life his chances of being successful are almost nil.

Has a fear of taking a risk ever caused you to protect yourself by inaction? If so, write your experiences below:

#5 TO ESCAPE

Juanita generally reacts in one of two ways when she's confronted by an unpleasant task. She will either struggle to complete it, or she'll try to get away from it. She almost always uses procrastination as her means of escape.

Juanita can be pretty aggressive in completing a task if she's under a lot of pressure. However her aggressive behavior isn't universally accepted by the people she has to work with.

Her co-workers have encouraged her to use reason and compromise to come up with acceptable solutions. However reason, compromise, and negotiation require skills that Juanita sometimes finds hard to muster. Therefore, whenever she's faced with an unpleasant personal confrontation, she'll either be aggressive or she'll procrastinate.

Juanita can't escape from the deadlines for completing those tasks even though she can sometimes escape from the unpleasant emotions that surround them. So, in spite of her delaying tactics, her stress, tension, and anxiety will continue to grow until her tasks are completed and her deadlines are gone.

Juanita must continue to search for ways of finishing her tasks. Otherwise, she'll just compound the conditions that made her escape in the first place.

Have you procrastinated to escape an unpleasant situation or task? If so, please record what happened in the space provided.

MAJOR CAUSES OF PROCRASTINATION (Continued)

#6 ANXIETY AND DEPRESSION

Anxiety is a sense of fear, apprehension, or painfulness of mind. It usually occurs over an impending or anticipated misfortune. It is both the cause and effect of Daniel's procrastination.

Daniel sometimes gets confused about reality and his ability to deal with the challenges of everyday living. His anxiety comes in response to real or imagined threats in his environment. Anticipated criticism, the fear of failure, or the possibility of an unhappy confrontation contribute to his state of despair.

Daniel avoids dealing with his threats by procrastinating. All this does is increase his anxiety because he knows he should be doing something and feels guilty when he doesn't do it. This is especially true when he sees how important a task is. At this point, his anxiety becomes a byproduct of his procrastination and is not caused by his fear of external factors.

Anxiety is a fairly common condition. A majority of people experience anxiety from time to time in their lives. It usually comes and goes as conditions change. When anxiety continues for long periods of time, it can easily turn into depression. This is a far more serious cause of procrastination.

Depression is a neurotic condition characterized by dejection and despair. In depression, people feel incapable of doing anything about the things that bother them. It's a condition that very often leads to Daniel's procrastination, and it's a tough one to overcome.

When Daniel gets depressed, he neglects most everything he should be doing. It's hard for him to make decisions of any kind because he feels so helpless.

Depression causes psychological fatigue. Daniel uses this as an additional excuse for procrastinating. It's ironic that one of the very best ways for him to get over his depression is to participate in some strenuous physical activity that he can control and enjoy. However Daniel is so lethargic when he's depressed that he just can't seem to get started in the kinds of activities that would help him the most.

Daniel may need professional help from a counselor or psychologist if his depression becomes severe. Being depressed, he'll probably postpone that too.

In spite of its gloomy nature, depression can be eliminated along with the procrastination that goes with it. Though it's not easy, it can be done.

Have you had experiences similar to Daniel? If so, take a minute and describe them below:

MAJOR CAUSES OF
PROCRASTINATION (Continued)

#7 OBSESSIVE/COMPULSIVE BEHAVIOR

Marcel is a perfectionist. He works hard, but gets very little done because he procrastinates until he's sure the outcome will be flawless.

This obsessive habit of doing—but not finishing—shields Marcel from criticism. If someone else finds fault in his efforts, he can always say he's "working on it."

Most people accept mistakes as a natural part of growth and development. Marcel sees mistakes of any kind as devastating indictments of personal weakness. That's why he procrastinates.

Elizabeth on the other hand is a compulsive procrastinator. She stays in constant motion in order to convey to others the impression that she's very busy. She also spends a lot of time doing things without getting any of it done.

Elizabeth feels compelled to take on an excessive number of tasks and often starts new ones before finishing the old ones. She's reluctant to finish anything because, like Marcel, she is afraid of being criticized. So, she continues to procrastinate and adds more tasks to those she already has.

Do the above situations sound familiar? Please spend some time describing experiences you have had that might be considered compulsive or obsessive that caused you to procrastinate:

#8 MONOTONY AND BOREDOM

A task is monotonous if it's tedious, uninteresting, lacks variety, and offers no rewards or incentives. If Chin sees it that way, he'll procrastinate about getting a task done until someone else does something to change its fundamental characteristics.

Chin sometimes thinks a job is monotonous when it's not. This is usually the case when he doesn't understand *why* it should be done. In order to keep from postponing his work, Chin has to see the benefits that can come from its completion. His perception of the job needs to be changed so he will recognize and accept the interesting characteristics that are inherent in the task he has been assigned.

Boredom is another cause of procrastination. But unlike monotony, which is due to the inherent characteristics of a task, boredom is due to the way people react to it. If they fail to see any benefits in a task, they're going to be bored.

Amy procrastinates because she's bored. She gets weary and dissatisfied, frequently suffers psychological fatigue, and takes no interest in the things she's supposed to be doing. She often uses her subjective state of exhaustion as an excuse for procrastinating.

Tasks can be changed to make them more interesting. The only way Amy's boredom can be eliminated is by changing her attitude toward the work she is expected to do.

Enthusiasm and energy can help relieve boredom. Fatigue can promote it.

When was the last time this happened to you? Write your response below:

MAJOR CAUSES OF
PROCRASTINATION (Continued)

#9 FATIGUE

Physical and psychological fatigue are major causes of procrastination. Physical fatigue can come from hard labor, lack of sleep, overexertion, or nervous exhaustion. When Steven is physically fatigued because of working two jobs, he still has an interest in doing each job. However it's hard to maintain his normal productivity because he lacks the energy needed to continue. He procrastinates because he's tired.

Steven's psychological fatigue reflects many of the same symptoms—exhaustion, weariness, and lack of energy—that are evident in his physical fatigue. But his psychological fatigue comes from boredom, apathy, or a lack of interest, not from working too hard.

The difference between Steven's physical and psychological fatigue is especially important when he wants to stop procrastinating. He can reduce his physical fatigue through rest and relaxation. His psychological fatigue will require rest and relaxation, as well as a change in his motivation toward the tasks to which he has been assigned.

All of us become fatigued. When was the last time fatigue caused you to put off a task?

#10 OUTSIDE FORCES

Heather knows she procrastinates because of conditions she brings on herself. And she knows she can usually stop procrastinating if she makes a decision to control these conditions. It's a lot harder for her to break the habit when her delays are caused by external pressures that she can't control.

Pressure can come from her clients, co-workers, supervisor, or family, and it can be immediate or extend over long periods of time. This very easily steers her in directions she would rather avoid.

She postponed her marriage in the face of parental opposition. She postponed her vacations because her employer said she was needed. She also has postponed a career change because her husband didn't want her to increase her time away from home.

Heather will have a hard time taking command of her own behavior as long as she allows external pressures to control her. She'll continue to procrastinate until she's able to identify the sources of the pressure, devise ways of regaining control, and begin taking charge of her own life.

Do outside forces keep you from what you want or need to accomplish? Please explain what they are in the space provided.

MAJOR CAUSES OF PROCRASTINATION (Continued)

#11 LACK OF ANALYTICAL ABILITY

Whenever Michael runs into a problem with his job, he has a hard time figuring out how to solve it. Since he's never really analyzed what he does, he tends to reject every possible answer that comes to his mind. He procrastinates because he's afraid that nothing he does will solve the problem. At the same time, he never takes the time to look for alternatives.

Michael usually procrastinates right up to a deadline. Then he scrambles to complete his task in the little time that remains. Sometimes, just when he thinks he's reached his goal, he suddenly discovers a better solution. If it's too late to start over, he winds up doing a poor job and wishes he could have done things differently.

After a while, Michael may catch on to what he is doing. But then he may procrastinate even more because he'll be afraid of making the same mistakes in the future.

Have you ever been afraid you will be unable to solve a problem because of a lack of analytical ability? Please describe your experiences below:

#12 FORGETFULNESS

Salvatore says he doesn't procrastinate, he just forgets to do certain things. If he *really* forgot a task, he wouldn't remember anything about it. He wouldn't even recognize the task when it was right in front of him.

It's possible that Salvatore has forgotten some of the things he should have been working on. More likely, he was procrastinating by consciously or subconsiously ignoring the job to which he was assigned.

Salvatore knew what he was supposed to do and when he was supposed to do it. Instead of going to work on it, he mentally set it aside. When asked if his task was done, he often responds by saying, "I completely forgot about it."

Salvatore will generally get flustered when someone else mentions a job that he has shelved in some remote corner of his subconscious. As long as nobody brings them up, he'll continue to procrastinate and let uncompleted jobs lie unattended.

Are you forgetful? Has it ever caused you to put things off? Please write your experiences below.

MAJOR CAUSES OF
PROCRASTINATION (Continued)

#13 DEPENDENCE ON OTHERS

Sue-Lin doesn't do much of anything for herself. She'd rather rely on the skill, strength, or knowledge of others to get her work done. She regularly postpones significant tasks until someone helps her or does the work for her. She turns to others because she doesn't think she can fend for herself. Sometimes she'll admit her dependence, but in most cases, she will deny it.

Sue-Lin is not unique. Executives often will postpone important letters or reports until a favorite secretary returns from vacation. Sales representatives will postpone sales calls until their manager can go with them. Supervisors will wait to discipline their employees until the boss is in the office.

As long as Sue-Lin is successful in getting help from others, she'll follow a regular pattern of dependent behavior as long as it pays off. She will quit procrastinating only when she sees the advantages of independence and develops a desire to do things for herself.

Does dependence on others cause you to procrastinate? Write out any situations that relate to this problem in the space provided.

#14 MANIPULATION OF OTHERS

Juan turns to others for help as a means of gaining a personal advantage. His procrastination is actually a deliberate attempt to manipulate other people.

People who share responsibility for Juan getting his work done usually lose their patience over his failure to do anything to help. If Juan senses their frustration and impatience, he'll keep delaying until they step in and take over. This not only allows Juan to avoid working on a task but also lets him escape responsibility for the end result.

People, in general, will avoid being manipulated as much as possible. Many of them are taken in by procrastinators, like Juan, who are able to recognize and take advantage of their willingness to step in and help do a job. Strangely enough, if an important task is at stake, many people will still help the procrastinator even when they don't want to. Worst of all, when help is finally refused, procrastinators like Juan will just go look for another pigeon.

We hope you don't manipulate others. If you do (as a means of procrastination) describe when and where this has occurred in the past.

MAJOR CAUSES OF
PROCRASTINATION (Continued)

#15 PHYSICAL DISABILITIES

Michelle procrastinates when she thinks she's physically incapable of doing a particular task. She'll use illness, injury, or a specific ailment like a bad back, poor eyesight, or lack of strength as her reason for delay. She'll continue to procrastinate until all evidence of her physical disability is eliminated.

Michelle compounds her procrastination by failing to correct her disabilities. She avoids physical labor because of back pain, but also will put off going to a doctor for treatment. Or she'll complain about eyestrain, but postpone a trip to an optometrist for new glasses.

People with legitimate disabilities feel badly about not being able to work. Procrastinators feel guilty and wish they knew how to change their behavior. Malingerers don't feel bad at all. They only pretend to be upset. They use their real or imagined disabilities as reasons for avoiding work of any kind. They have neither the intention nor the desire to eliminate their disabilities as long as personal benefits can be realized from their inactivity.

Have you ever used tactics similar to those of Michelle to avoid doing a task? Describe what you have done below:

ADD YOUR OWN

The fifteen reasons why people procrastinate listed on the preceeding pages may not have included your ''pet'' reason. Please describe it (and any others) in the space below:

I procrastinate by:

COMING UP

You've just covered fifteen different reasons why people procrastinate. As you read through them, you probably recognized some you had listed back on page 9. The comparison between your list and the list shown on page 10, will help you better understand why you do what you do. It will also help you start planning on how you can get rid of this habit. At the least, you now know you're just like lots of other people who have trouble with delays and postponements. By comparing your list with the fifteen reasons identified in this section, you've started to analyze your behavior. That's a big step forward.

The next section describes eighteen specific techniques that will help you stop procrastinating. After you read Section III, you can match the techniques you think will work best against the causes that bother you most. Learn how to: conquer your fears if fear is a problem, boost your ego if you're depressed subdivide if complex tasks frustrate you, and if you come up with suggestions that aren't listed, that's great! Write them down where you won't forget them. Then go ahead and use them whenever you can.

As you work through the descriptions of causes and cures, beginning on page 33, you'll start experiencing the satisfaction of getting things done. You'll gain momentum as you go along, and if you're like most people, you'll start having fun and enjoying yourself. Before you know it, with practice, procrastination will be a thing of the past. So commit now to carefully read Section III and learn how you can have a more satisfying and rewarding life.

ON TO SECTION III!

SECTION III

HOW TO STOP PROCRASTINATING

NOW. **Right this minute is the best time to stop procrastinating.** Think for a moment of all the important things you've been putting off—the letters and reports you should have written, the phone calls you should have made, projects you should have completed, or the books you should have read. Turn the page and write them down.

HOW TO STOP PROCRASTINATING

THINGS I'VE BEEN POSTPONING:

Letters to Send: _____

Reports to Write: _____

Calls to Make: _____

Projects to Complete: _____

Books to Read: _____

Exercises to Do: _____

Habits to Break: _____

Why haven't I been doing these things? _____

MY REASONS FOR PROCRASTINATING:

1. _____

2. _____

3. _____

4. _____

5. _____

Compare your list of things you should be doing with your reasons for not doing them. If the things you should be doing are really important, then there's no way you're going to reconcile the two lists.

GET OFF YOUR DUFF!

Stop procrastinating right now and do one single thing that relates to each of the tasks you have on your "postponed" list.

1. Get out a pad and pencil.
2. Look up a phone number.
3. Pick up the book.
4. Do one sit up.
5. Put out your cigarette.
6. Get rid of your candy bar.
7. Skip your before dinner drink.

ADD YOUR OWN:

8. _____

9. _____

10. _____

YOU CAN'T DO IT?

You say you can't do your report until you get your typewriter fixed? You learned to write before you learned to type, so start writing—or throw your typewriter in the car and drive it to a repair shop.

You say you need to buy a scale before you start dieting? Wear your tight fitting skirt or trousers. When they fit better, you'll know you've lost weight.

Go back to your reasons for goofing off and see if they're really as tough as you think they are.

Sometimes you will have to eliminate a bad habit or change some other pattern of behavior before you can stop procrastinating and start being more successful. You might have to give up the coffee breaks you take every morning and afternoon, especially if they're ill-timed or serve no useful purpose. Or you might have to change your TV watching habits if the programs you watch no longer stimulate, interest, or amuse you.

GET GOING NOW!

SUGGESTIONS TO STOP PROCRASTINATING

Now you're primed and ready to go. Start working on the eighteen suggestions that are listed below and described in this section. Some of them deal with the way you behave. Others relate to situations you find yourself in. Decide which suggestions will help the most and get started on them right away. Come back to the others as you gain confidence and things start getting done.

Add to the list of suggestions in this book whenever you can. Build your own workbook for getting things done. This is just a start on your journey toward success. Turn the page for the first step.

STOP PROCRASTINATING—GET TO WORK! BY:

1. BEING HAPPY
2. KNOWING YOURSELF
3. CONQUERING YOUR FEARS
4. REWARDING YOURSELF
5. SUBDIVIDING YOUR DUTIES
6. ORGANIZING AND PLANNING BETTER
7. SETTING PRIORITIES
8. MANAGING YOUR TIME
9. DELEGATING MORE
10. SEEKING DIVERSIONS
11. EXERCISING YOUR MIND
12. ANALYZING YOUR REASONS FOR PROCRASTINATION
13. BECOMING MORE DECISIVE
14. MAKING A COMMITMENT
15. LAUNCHING A LEADING TASK
16. VISUALIZING COMPLETION
17. BEING IMPARTIAL
18. REGULATING YOUR ENVIRONMENT

ADD YOUR OWN:

19. _____

20. _____

SUGGESTIONS (Continued)

> **#1 BE HAPPY**

The way you feel about the things you need to do will greatly affect the way you do them. If you're happy, they will be done sooner and you'll have fewer problems and be able to enjoy the happiness of the people around you. If you're angry or dissatisfied, your work will drag on, you'll make more mistakes, and the people you work with will go out of their way to avoid you.

If you want to get rid of a bad habit, you have to change the attitudes that led to the development of that habit in the first place.*

Accentuate the positive. Turn your unhappy thoughts around and think about how good you'll feel when you get done.

Being happy is easy. As Abraham Lincoln said, ''You're about as happy as you make up your mind to be.''

If you're having a hard time cracking a smile, then try these suggestions. They're guaranteed to help.

1. Look for happy things in your environment. Stay away from the obituaries, political news, and disaster reports in your newspaper and spend more time with the comics.

2. Read happy books, and put those that are full of murder and mayhem back on the shelf.

3. Go to happy movies, or rent an old one that tickled your funny bone years ago.

4. Laugh at things you think are funny.

Spread your happiness to other people. They'll be more than happy to share your joy and help you on your road to success.

---

*Don't procrastinate. Order *Attitude: Your Most Priceless Possession* using the form in the back of this book.

SUGGESTIONS (Continued)

#2 KNOW YOURSELF

Take a minute and answer these questions:

What are my capabilities?

What are my limitations?

What levels of achievement are open to me?

What are my goals and objectives? Are they realistically attainable?

What have been my major successes?

What have been my failures?

What lies ahead in my future?

How do I compare with other people, especially those with whom I've been competing for success?

Learn to recognize and understand your moods. They are your conscious states of mind and determine which emotions control your behavior. Make a point of recognizing which ones help you and which ones cause you to procrastinate. Make your moods work for you, not against you.

Stay away from volatile situations if you're in a lousy mood. Tackle the hard parts of your job when you're in a productive or energetic mood.

Change your mood before going to work on a project, especially if it's going to make you procrastinate. But don't spend all day working on your moods, or you'll lose sight of the job you're supposed to be doing.

SUGGESTIONS (Continued)

#3 CONQUER YOUR FEARS

Fears live in the dark corners and hidden recesses of your mind. Most of them will wither and die if you drag them out into the open and meet them head-on.

Don't fuss and fret over fears that lie somewhere in the distant future. Work on the problems that you have to face today, especially those that make you procrastinate.

List three major things you think could go wrong with your job.

Problem #1:
Problem #2:
Problem #3:

How would you handle each problem if it were the only thing you had to worry about?

Solution #1:
Solution #2:
Solution #3:

Force yourself to do this little exercise whenever you start worrying about your job. You'll be surprised to find that often your fears will disappear in a flash.

Here's how this exercise works in real life. You want to ask your boss for a raise, but you're afraid that you'll be chewed out and maybe even let go for asking. That's problem #1.

Here are your solutions.

Solution #1: Review your worth to the company—list contributions you have made.
Solution # 2: Update your resume.
Solution # 3: Line up some interviews.
Solution # 4: Sharpen your negotiating skills.*
Solution # 5: Find out everything you can about comparable jobs, including salary ranges.
Solution # 6: Prepare to ask for what you think is fair compensation.
Solution # 7: Arrange to meet with your boss and ask for your raise, assuming you feel it is deserved, based on the research you have done.

Even the worst possible outcome (which is not likely) can be adapted to, if it's faced head on.

---

*For an excellent book on this subject, order *Successful Negotiation* using the form in the back of this book.

SUGGESTIONS (Continued)

#4 REWARD YOURSELF

If you procrastinate because you lack motivation, are depressed, or feel sorry for yourself, then you have a major rebuilding job ahead of you.

Start by giving yourself a pep talk. Remind yourself that you're a good and capable person. Give yourself credit where credit is due. Acknowledge your skills and strengths. Counter criticism from others with a list of your best accomplishments.

Reward yourself when you do a good job. Feed your self-esteem* with the pleasure that comes from getting things done. Assign points to the jobs you have to do. Give yourself more points for hard tasks than for easy ones. Give yourself bonus points for exceeding your standards.

Your rewards can be simple and inexpensive, but they should be things that will help you stop procrastinating and give you the motivation you need to be successful.

A meal at a special restaurant, a night at the movies, or sleeping late are examples of things you can use as rewards as long as you really enjoy them. Just remember that a reward system only works when you strictly adhere to it. So, if you earn a reward, take it. And if you don't earn it, don't take it. Don't diminish your accomplishments by thinking they are not worth the rewards you set aside for them.

*Don't procrastinate! Order *Developing Self-Esteem* using the form in the back of this book.

#5 SUBDIVIDE

Subdivide your job if you think it's complicated. Cut it up into little pieces and concentrate on how it's put together. You'll probably find that it is a lot less complicated than you first thought.

Write down the subtasks. If you do a thorough job of subdividing, you should be able to complete many subtasks in just a few minutes. Then check each off as it is completed. You'll get a lot more done and it will be easier to do.

The enthusiasm you'll experience in completing the tasks and checking them off your list will speed you toward your goal and give you a sense of accomplishment.

If you run into a dead end along the way, stop. Direct your efforts to a different aspect of the job until the hurdle clears. Thinking about and completing something else will give your mind a refreshing break. When you go back to your original problem, you'll probably have a solution that might have been lost if you had simply sat and worried about it.

Subdividing is particularly effective for unpleasant jobs, because almost anyone can do something they dislike if they only have to do it for a short time.

Break down the tough, complicated tasks into small subtasks. Spread them out and fill in time between with things you like to do. It may take a little longer, but you'll feel a lot better when you're done.

If you can't break down your job, then subdivide the time you spend working on it. Put everything else out of your mind and concentrate on what you have to do for 15 minutes. When the time is up, stop and go on to something else. Give your mind a break. Then come back a little later and work on your task again for another 15 minutes. Then leave it again. Keep doing this until you're finished.

SUGGESTIONS (Continued)

#6 ORGANIZE AND PLAN

The best way to stop procrastinating is to never do it in the first place. You can accomplish this enviable trait by organizing your work ahead of time and planning how you're going to get it done.

A job well-defined is a job half done. The more time you spend in planning, the less time you'll need for doing.

Start the planning process by setting some long-term goals and objectives.

Goals are idealistic, hoped-for accomplishments that can be established almost anytime. They are general statements from which specific objectives can be developed.

EXAMPLE: "I need to lose weight"

Objectives are clear statements of things you want to do in specified time periods. A good objective is one you can measure so you'll know for sure if you've reached it.

EXAMPLE: "I will start today and lose seven pounds within a three-week period."

Make a checklist of everything you need to do to accomplish your goals and objectives. Avoid cluttering up your list with busywork. Make sure you're zeroing in on things that will lead to a successful future. Do this the first thing in the morning or the last thing the night before. Assign priorities to your tasks so you'll be sure of doing the important things first.

Take time to reflect at the end of each day. Look at your work list and see how well you did. Incorporate your insights about today into your plans for tomorrow.

ORGANIZE AND PLAN (Continued)

Fill in spare time with special tasks. If you're always coming up short at the end of the day, spread your tasks over a longer time period.

Build some measure of improvement into your expectations, and try to do a little better every day.*

Don't become preoccupied with method, technique, and procedure or you'll lose sight of the entire process. Be goal oriented. Focus on your objectives and move briskly toward their completion. Take shortcuts when you see them, and don't hesitate to throw out any incidental tasks that get in your way. Don't just think about doing things; think about getting things done.

---

*For an excellent book on this subject, order *Successful Self-Management* using the form in the back of this book.

SUGGESTIONS (Continued)

#7 SET PRIORITIES

Arrange your tasks in order of priority and then do all the important things first.

Here are the categories that Edwin Bliss, the well-respected consultant, recommends:

1. **Important and Urgent.** These are the tasks that should be at the top of your list. Do them right away or you'll suffer serious consequences.

2. **Important But Not Urgent.** These tasks should be near the top, but most people ignore them because they can be postponed. They include things like making a spontaneous sales call, writing a letter to a client, or giving a favorable performance review to a co-worker.

3. **Urgent But Not Important.** These tasks tend to be high on other people's lists. If you put them ahead of your high priority tasks, you're probably looking for approval from others. Making coffee for the boss is probably the worst of the lot.

4. **Busy Work.** These tasks can provide a welcome relief from difficult tasks if you control them. Yet spending too much time on them is just another form of procrastination.

5. **Wasted Time.** This group of tasks should be excluded from your list of priorities.

Keep your goals and objectives in front of you, and do what's necessary to get them done. Reexamine your priorities from time to time so you know you're on the right track. Feel free to change your priorities if it looks like things aren't going the way they should. Be determined to say "no" to tasks that can be disruptive.

SUGGESTIONS (Continued)

#8 MANAGE YOUR TIME

The distance between *being late* and *being too late* is like the difference between being struck by a lightning bug, and being struck by lightning.

Some of your work must be done by a certain date. Examples include the end of the fiscal year, the start of a reporting period, or ''tax time.'' If you sit on your hands and procrastinate, you'll miss these crucial deadlines.

Other tasks, like prospecting for new clients, can be done almost any time, but they still must be done and need deadlines. Know what those deadlines are and know how to work with them.

Time needs to be budgeted like any other valuable resource. If you waste time, it is lost forever.

You can replace the money you lost because of a poor investment by working longer and harder. You can regain knowledge you lost by studying and relearning. You can usually regain your lost health through diet, exercise and/or the help of a physician. However when you lose time, it is gone forever. You can never get it back.

There are countless times during a day when, with some planning, you can complete simple tasks. If you're waiting somewhere for something to happen, become productive. Write a note to yourself of things you want to accomplish that week or write a letter to someone. You can also use this time productively for meditation or relaxation.

Parkinson's Law says that work will expand to fill the time available. On the other hand, if you make less time available for unimportant tasks, you should be able to get rid of useless activity and wasted effort.

Know your deadlines and stick with them. Keep a tight schedule that prevents dawdling and procrastination. Acknowledge success along the way and reward yourself for doing a good job. It will keep you going at a steady pace.

SUGGESTIONS (Continued)

#9 DELEGATE

If you're overwhelmed by the complexity of your job, you should divide it into clearly defined elements. Then give parts of it to other people.

Make sure the people to whom you've delegated a task understand the interrelationships of the subtasks. If they are confused, they will procrastinate and you'll get back more work than you gave out. Provide lots of information at the beginning. If they completely understand what is expected they won't keep coming back for clarification.

Once you've delegated full responsibility for several subtasks, you'll be free to work on the parts you kept. Combine the results as required until you end up with a final product. You'll be surprised at how easy it is to get even a complex assignment completed. Best of all, you'll make other people happy by having them contribute to a worthwhile task. Be sure to recognize their contributions appropriately, or next time you delegate they may not be nearly as enthusiastic!

HE NEEDS TO LEARN TO DELEGATE

#10 SEEK DIVERSIONS

Sometimes it helps to take a break from a difficult task. Just be sure you've kept track of your progress and know exactly where you left off. Then you won't be as likely to procrastinate about restarting.

Walking or jogging or other similar physical activity is an especially effective diversion. The exercise will clear your mind, stimulate your heart and give you energy to finish your task. The sights and sounds you'll encounter can help you generate new ideas or approaches to your task.

Take some time off. Read a book. Rest and relaxation help to restore bodily processes, reduce physical fatigue and allow your subconscious thoughts to generate new and effective solutions to nagging problems.

SUGGESTIONS (Continued)

#11 EXERCISE YOUR MIND

It is time for some mental aerobics. Practice these simple exercises every day and you'll develop more brain power, get more done, and do your job better than you ever thought possible.

1. **Contemplate:** Think about the mental aspects of your job. Use your sense of taste, touch, smell, sight, or sound to create vivid images of the things your job requires. Taste them, touch them, smell them, see them, hear them. Consume the pleasures of your senses, by noticing the smell of the office coffee pot or watching the mail person carry off a report you have completed. Reflect on your position in your organization and appreciate its good features.

2. **Study:** Learn something new every day. Learn something that will help you get ahead in your job, or something you've always wanted to know. Learn about your business. Study the products and services of your competitors. Master a new technology that will contribute to your success.

3. **Reflect:** Events of your past can give fullness to the present and the future. Start a journal by documenting your work history. Note trends and developments in your profession. Record your accomplishments. Talk to people who have traveled the pathways you're now trying to master.

4. **Initiate Action:** Do something that requires initiative and imagination. Make a cold-call on a prospect. Send a friendly note to a valued client. Solve a problem that keeps pestering you. Take more chances.

EXERCISE YOUR MIND (Continued)

5. **Achieve:** Wrap up an aspect of your job that you've been neglecting. Finish a task before it's due. Schedule a vacation you've always wanted to take but postponed because you were ''too busy.'' Clean out your ''in'' basket.

6. **Create:** Give something to the world that will last beyond your lifetime. Develop a new product, policy, service, or procedure that will be around after you leave your position.

The more involved you are with your work, the less likely you'll be to procrastinate about doing it.

YOUR ABILITY TO GET INVOLVED IS LIMITED ONLY BY YOUR IMAGINATION.

SUGGESTIONS (Continued)

#12 ANALYZE YOUR REASONS FOR PROCRASTINATING

Lack of knowledge can cause apathy, and apathy is a forerunner of procrastination. You can conquer apathy and procrastination by learning as much as possible about the things you have to do.

Go back to page 9 and analyze your reasons for postponing a task. Then compare those reasons with the reasons you—or other people—have for getting the job done.

If you can come up with more good reasons for delaying a job than doing it, then drop that job and go on to something else. It doesn't make sense for you to hang on to an unimportant task if it causes you anxiety or frustration and makes you procrastinate.

If the job has been assigned to you by someone else, then you'd better do it even though you'd like to postpone it. If you still find it impossible to do, you may have to reconsider your relationship with the other person. In extreme cases, this could mean quitting a job or ending a friendship. If you've carefully analyzed your task, the correct choice should be fairly easy, and you should know what to do.

If your job is worth doing, it's worth knowing about. Do some research if you're uncertain about your facts. Then search for more information to provide the momentum you need to get off to a good start.

The more you learn, the more you will want to know. By applying your new knowledge as you learn it, you'll finish your task in less time and have fewer problems.

Share your knowledge with others and involve them in your work. They'll absorb your enthusiasm and support your efforts to get things done.

#13 BE DECISIVE

Go to work on a task as soon as you have everything you need to get started. Forget about the contingencies that might occur. Make adjustments as you go. If you find out later that you've made a mistake, admit it and start over.

Make up your mind early to go ahead with a task or leave it. Act without reservation or regret. If you prolong your decision, you're just procrastinating in a different way. Be responsible for your decision and avoid the anxiety and indecision that comes from continued procrastination.

SUGGESTIONS (Continued)

#14 MAKE A COMMITMENT

You will have a far greater chance of getting a job done if you not only commit yourself to doing it, but also share your commitment with people you feel good about. Share your commitment with your co-workers, your friends, and your employer. You'll naturally start thinking more about your commitment to them and worry less about your own self-interests.

People with whom you share a commitment can help you by setting deadlines, reviewing your progress toward a goal, or evaluating your results. Your fears and anxieties will become secondary to their expectations, and sharing your accomplishments with other people will make them all seem a lot more enjoyable.

#15 LAUNCH A LEADING TASK

A leading task is one that breaks the ice and gets you involved in a larger task that you've been putting off. A leading task should be a relatively simple task that requires little planning or conscious effort on your part.

A leading task can be as simple as sharpening your pencil, inserting a sheet of paper in the typewriter, or looking up the phone number of a customer. On the other hand, it can be more involved, like scheduling an appointment with a client, or a performance review with a co-worker.

A leading task will be successful only if it launches you on a course of action that overcomes your procrastination. Otherwise, a simple task like clearing off your desk may amount to nothing more than busy work.

SUGGESTIONS (Continued)

#16 VISUALIZE COMPLETION

You can do any job faster and better if you can see yourself completing it. The key lies in the intensity of your vision and the depth of your concentration.

Try this little exercise. Start by clearing your mind of stressful thoughts. Think only about the job you've been putting off. Then try to get a good visual image in your mind's eye of the steps needed to complete your task. See yourself carrying out those steps. Picture yourself with the end-product in hand.

If you've concentrated very hard on completing each step, the picture you formed will motivate you to act right away. As long as you can see something being done, you'll be motivated to do it. If the picture is clear, and you still don't act, you'll begin feeling uncomfortable, then anxious, and finally frustrated about not getting on with the job work.

If you're too close to your task to see it being completed, just stand back and take a detached look. Or get someone to help you; they may see a solution that you've missed.

#17 BE IMPARTIAL

Outside influences can bring about both procrastination and unnecessary anxiety. Especially if you have to complete a task in the face of a personality conflict.

If you procrastinate because of the way other people feel toward you, you're letting them control your life. This not only keeps you from reaching your goals and objectives, it also will cause you a lot of anxiety. It's your life to live. To do it successfully, you cannot let outsiders interfere.

Be tactful and considerate of other people's opinions. Treat everyone equally and try to keep them happy. Come to terms with potential adversaries before your work begins by diffusing any conflicts that may exist. If your attempts at mediation are unsuccessful, then just bite the bullet and forge ahead in spite of outside criticism and complaints.

SUGGESTIONS (Continued)

#18 REGULATE YOUR ENVIRONMENT

Your procrastination may be due to noise, poor lighting, temperature that is too hot or too cold, or other physical distractions. If this is the case, then change your environment.

Determine what kind of environment is best for your productivity. Experiment with different levels of noise and light intensity. Work alone or with others. Work early in the day, late at night, or at midday. Work right before or right after strenuous exercise. Keep track of your results. This will allow you to identify optimum times and conditions when you're at your best.

This is the last of the eighteen suggestions to help you break the habit of procrastination. As you went through them, other suggestions may have come to mind. We hope you wrote them down. Now that you have seen the causes of procrastination and read about suggestions to stop procrastinating, it is time to put them together into a plan of action. That's the subject of the next, and final section.

SECTION IV

YOUR PLAN OF ACTION?

Yesterday is only a dream, you'll never get it back. Tomorrow is only a vision, it can't be guaranteed. But, today is real and if you live it with heart and soul from beginning to end, yesterday will become a dream of accomplishment and tomorrow will become a vision of hope.

START PLANNING NOW!

You've taken some big steps since you started this journey. You've learned about some of the causes of procrastination, and discovered suggestions to help you break the procrastination habit.

You probably knew about some of what you read. Part of it may have been new to you, and some may have given you new ideas as you went along.

Now you have to sift through everything you have learned and come up with a plan of action that will serve your needs, meet your capabilities, and recognize your limitations. The final objective is to help you break the procrastination habit!

Your plan should contain elements of everything you've read. It should become a guide that will allow you to decide what has to be done and when and how you should do it. Once you have your plan of action put together, you will have to apply it, if it is to do you any good.

There are no magic wands or quick fixes to break old habits. If you want to stop procrastinating, you just have to do it. The good news is that with work, old habits can be broken, and new, more positive ones, learned.

STEPS TO COMPLETE MY PLAN

HERE AND NOW (Continued)

Get started on your plan as soon as you finish this book. Clear your desk, table, floor, or workbench of everything except the task you're putting off. Clear your mind of thoughts that don't relate to the task at hand. Then take immediate and decisive action.

If your goal is to start an exercise program, then get down on the floor and do 5 push ups and 5 situps or go for a walk. If you want to stop smoking, flush your cigarettes down the toilet. If you want to go on a diet, then give away all of the cookies and snacks in your cupboard and don't replace them. If you want to change jobs, pick up the phone and start making appointments to talk with others. If you have an exam coming up, get out your notes and start reviewing them. If you want to write a letter to a customer, address the envelope, put a sheet of stationary in the typewriter or computer and start typing.

If the task you choose is a positive one, it will break the shackles of inertia and send you speeding toward your goal. You'll feel you're on the way.

A single well-conceived act of your own choosing, such as saying ''no'' to a habitual temptation, or performing a productive act, will launch you on an accelerated level of activity. As you continue for days or weeks, you will enjoy a whole new range of power.

STOP PROCRASTINATING: GET TO WORK!

56

ESTABLISH A GOAL!

Describe your habit-breaking task in terms of a goal.

"By _____ (date) I will _____ (do something) in order to _____ (outcome)."

Divide up the weeks, days, or hours that lie ahead and assign the steps you have to take to achieve your goal to each time segment. Then take your first step. Later—today, tomorrow, next week, next hour, or next year—take step two, then step three, until you finish. As the well known Leo Hauser says, "By the yard it's hard, by the inch it's a cinch."

Focus on what you've accomplished, not how much there is left to do. Concentrate on developing a positive attitude and enhanced self-esteem and don't worry about developing slick techniques for getting there. If you feel good about yourself, the techniques will come along on their own.

Picture your essential goals and objectives in your mind's eye. Then with this book at your side, take off, move out, set sail, break camp, make tracks. Start doing all the important things that are out there waiting for you. Stay with your plan and recognize your achievements. Savor the excitement of growth and development. And relish the happiness that will come from your success.

NOTES

FOR OTHER FIFTY-MINUTE SELF-STUDY
BOOKS SEE THE BACK OF THE BOOK.

58

NOTES

$\boxed{\textbf{NOTES}}$

FOR OTHER FIFTY-MINUTE SELF-STUDY
BOOKS SEE THE BACK OF THE BOOK.

60

FOR OTHER FIFTY-MINUTE SELF-STUDY
BOOKS SEE THE BACK OF THE BOOK.

NOTES

FOR OTHER FIFTY-MINUTE SELF-STUDY
BOOKS SEE THE BACK OF THE BOOK.

NOTES

FOR OTHER FIFTY-MINUTE SELF-STUDY
BOOKS SEE THE BACK OF THE BOOK.

ABOUT THE FIFTY-MINUTE SERIES

We hope you enjoyed this book and found it valuable. If so, we have good news for you. This title is part of the best selling *FIFTY-MINUTE Series* of books. All other books are similar in size and identical in price. Several books are supported with a training video. These are identified by the symbol **V** next to the title.

Since the first *FIFTY-MINUTE* book appeared in 1986, more than five million copies have been sold worldwide. Each book was developed with the reader in mind. The result is a concise, high quality module written in a positive, readable self-study format.

FIFTY-MINUTE Books and Videos are available from your distributor or from Crisp Publications, Inc., 95 First Street, Los Altos, CA 94022. A free current catalog is available on request.

The complete list of *FIFTY-MINUTE Series* Books and Videos are listed on the following pages and organized by general subject area.

MANAGEMENT TRAINING

	Self-Managing Teams	00-0
	Delegating for Results	008-6
	Successful Negotiation — Revised	09-2
V	Increasing Employee Productivity	10-8
	Personal Performance Contracts — Revised	12-2
V	Team Building — Revised	16-5
V	Effective Meeting Skills	33-5
V	An Honest Day's Work: Motivating Employees	39-4
V	Managing Disagreement Constructively	41-6
	Learning To Lead	43-4
V	The Fifty-Minute Supervisor — 2/e	58-0
V	Leadership Skills for Women	62-9
V	Coaching & Counseling	68-8
	Ethics in Business	69-6
	Understanding Organizational Change	71-8

MANAGEMENT TRAINING (Cont.)

	Project Management	75-0
	Risk Taking	076-9
	Managing Organizational Change	80-7
V	Working Together in a Multi-Cultural Organization	85-8
	Selecting And Working With Consultants	87-4
	Empowerment	096-5
	Managing for Commitment	099-X
	Rate Your Skills as a Manager	101-5

PERSONNEL/HUMAN RESOURCES

V	Your First Thirty Days: A Professional Image in a New Job	003-5
	Office Management: A Guide to Productivity	005-1
	Men and Women: Partners at Work	009-4
	Effective Performance Appraisals — Revised	11-4
	Quality Interviewing — Revised	13-0
	Personal Counseling	14-9
	Giving and Receiving Criticism	023-X
	Attacking Absenteeism	042-6
	New Employee Orientation	46-7
	Professional Excellence for Secretaries	52-1
	Guide to Affirmative Action	54-8
	Writing a Human Resources Manual	70-X
	Downsizing Without Disaster	081-7
	Winning at Human Relations	86-6
	High Performance Hiring	088-4

COMMUNICATIONS

	Technical Writing in the Corporate World	004-3
V	Effective Presentation Skills	24-6
V	Better Business Writing — Revised	25-4
V	The Business of Listening	34-3
	Writing Fitness	35-1
	The Art of Communicating	45-9
	Technical Presentation Skills	55-6
V	Making Humor Work	61-0
	50 One Minute Tips to Better Communication	071-X
	Speed-Reading in Business	78-5
	Influencing Others	84-X

PERSONAL IMPROVEMENT

(v) Attitude: Your Most Priceless Possession — Revised   011-6
(v) Personal Time Management   22-X
Successful Self-Management   26-2
Business Etiquette And Professionalism   32-9
(v) Balancing Home & Career — Revised   35-3
(v) Developing Positive Assertiveness   38-6
The Telephone and Time Management   53-X
Memory Skills in Business   56-4
Developing Self-Esteem   66-1
Managing Personal Change   74-2
Finding Your Purpose   072-8
Concentration!   073-6
Plan Your Work/Work Your Plan!   078-7
Stop Procrastinating: Get To Work!   88-2
12 Steps to Self-Improvement   102-3

CREATIVITY

Systematic Problem Solving & Decision Making   63-7
(v) Creativity in Business   67-X
Intuitive Decision Making   098-1

TRAINING

Training Managers to Train   43-2
Visual Aids in Business   77-7
Developing Instructional Design   076-0
Training Methods That Work   082-5

WELLNESS

(v) Mental Fitness: A Guide to Stress Management   15-7
Wellness in the Workplace   020-5
Personal Wellness   21-3
Preventing Job Burnout   23-8
(v) Job Performance and Chemical Dependency   27-0
Overcoming Anxiety   29-9
Productivity at the Workstation   41-8
Health Strategies for Working Women   079-5

CUSTOMER SERVICE/SALES TRAINING

Sales Training Basics — Revised   02-5
Restaurant Server's Guide — Revised   08-4
Effective Sales Management   31-0
Professional Selling   42-4
Telemarketing Basics   60-2
Telephone Courtesy & Customer Service — Revised   64-7

CUSTOMER SERVICE/SALES TRAINING (CONT.)

(V) Calming Upset Customers — 65-3

(V) Quality at Work — 72-6

Managing Quality Customer Service — 83-1

Customer Satisfaction — Revised — 84-1

(V) Quality Customer Service — Revised — 95-5

SMALL BUSINESS/FINANCIAL PLANNING

Consulting for Success — 006-X

Understanding Financial Statements — 22-1

Marketing Your Consulting or Professional Services — 40-8

Starting Your New Business — 44-0

Direct Mail Magic — 075-2

Credits & Collections — 080-9

Publicity Power — 82-3

Writing & Implementing Your Marketing Plan — 083-3

Personal Financial Fitness — Revised — 89-0

Financial Planning With Employee Benefits — 90-4

ADULT LITERACY/BASIC LEARNING

Returning to Learning: Getting Your G.E.D. — 02-7

Study Skills Strategies — Revised — 05-X

The College Experience — 07-8

Basic Business Math — 24-8

Becoming an Effective Tutor — 28-0

Reading Improvement — 086-8

Introduction to Microcomputers — 087-6

Clear Writing — 094-9

Building Blocks of Business Writing — 095-7

Language, Customs & Protocol For Foreign Students — 097-3

CAREER BUILDING

Career Discovery - Revised — 07-6

Effective Networking — 30-2

Preparing for Your Interview — 33-7

Plan B: Protecting Your Career — 48-3

I Got The Job! - Revised — 59-9

Job Search That Works — 105-8

To order books/videos from the FIFTY-MINUTE Series, please:

1. **CONTACT YOUR DISTRIBUTOR**

   or

2. **Write to Crisp Publications, Inc.**
   95 First Street   **(415) 949-4888 - phone**
   Los Altos, CA 94022   **(415) 949-1610 - FAX**